I like You More Each Day

Written and Illustrated by

Andy Boerger

Published

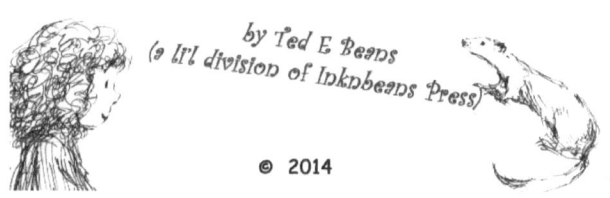
by Ted E Beans
(a lil division of Inknbeans Press)

© 2014

Cover art: Andy Boerger

© 2014   Andy Boerger and Ted E Beans (a li'l division of Inknbeans Press)

ISBN-13: 978-0615971834 (Ted E Beans)

ISBN-10: 0615971830

Table of Contents

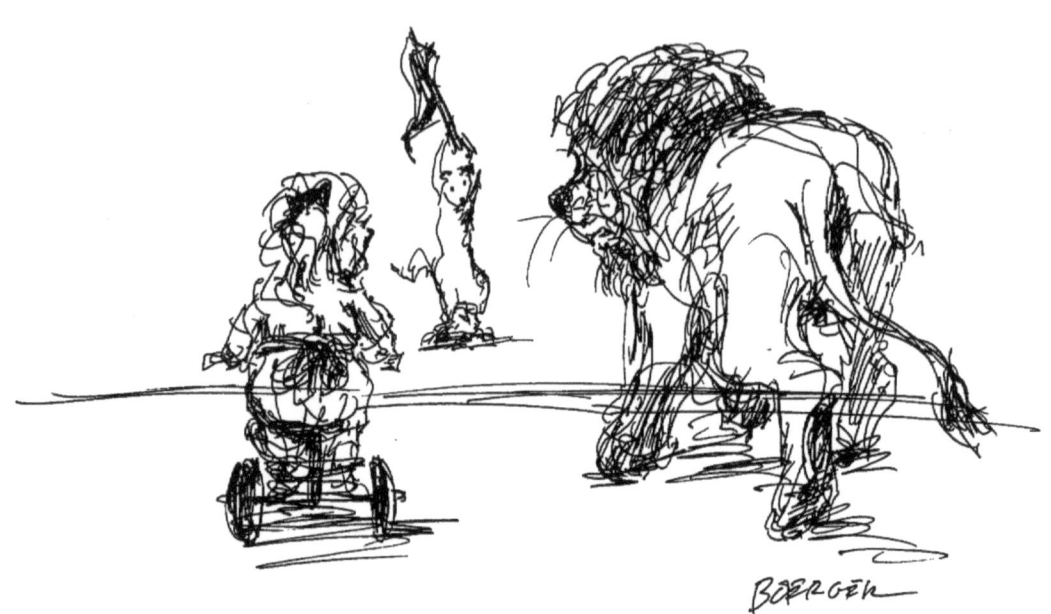

How Long Have We Been Friends?

How long have we been friends?
I don't think it's been long at all.
And where were you before then?
I'm not sure that I can recall.
But I must have been awfully small.

How long will we *stay* friends?
Well, I hope it will be many years,
since we've both of us just gotten here.
We have hundreds of games still to play,
and I like you more each day.

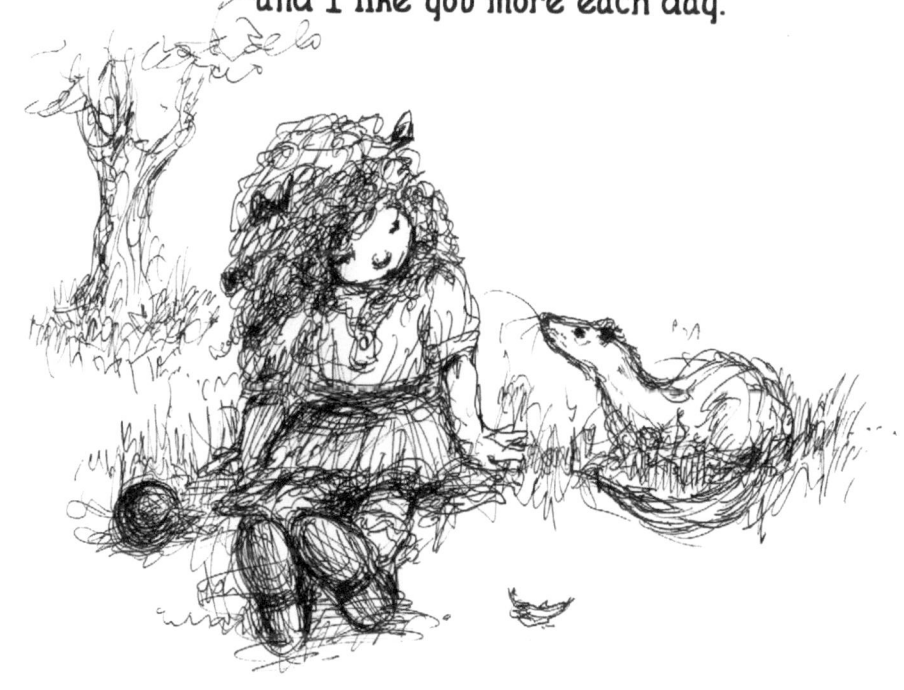

Bedly Day

This will be a bedly day.

What did you say? A bedly day?
You'll just lie in bed?

That's *not* what I said.
I'll move about, perhaps go out.
There are flowers to smell, after all.
But whenever I choose,
I'll come in for a snooze;
my bed will remain on call.

I like it!   You do?
Well, there's room here for two!
Let's share this bedly day.
Hooray!

BOERGER

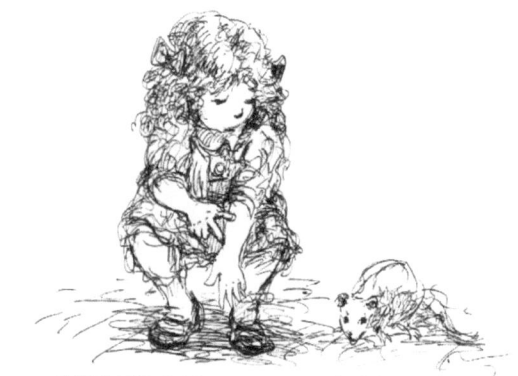

Seconds n' Minutes n' Hours n' Days
n' Weeks n' Months n' Years

Seconds n' Minutes n' Hours n' Days
n' Weeks n' Months n' Years
bustle along like a tidy line of ants upon a pier;
but watches n' clocks n' calendar talk's
no music to *these* ears,
for Life's best treasures will never be measured
in seconds or minutes or hours or days or weeks or months or years!

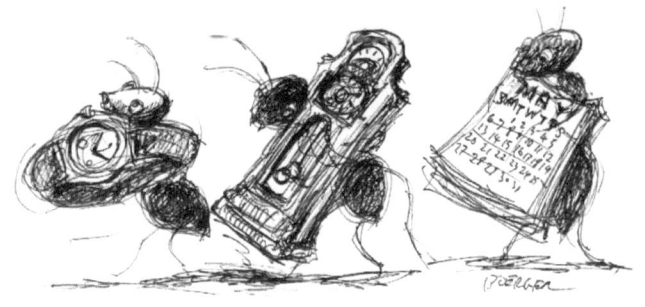

Brrr Cold

It isn't just cold today.
Why, it's downright brrr cold, I say!
'Brrr cold'? Absurd!
'Brrr' isn't a word!
So what if it's not?
I doubt that *you've* got
a righter way to say
how cold it is today!

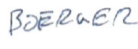

BOERGER

4

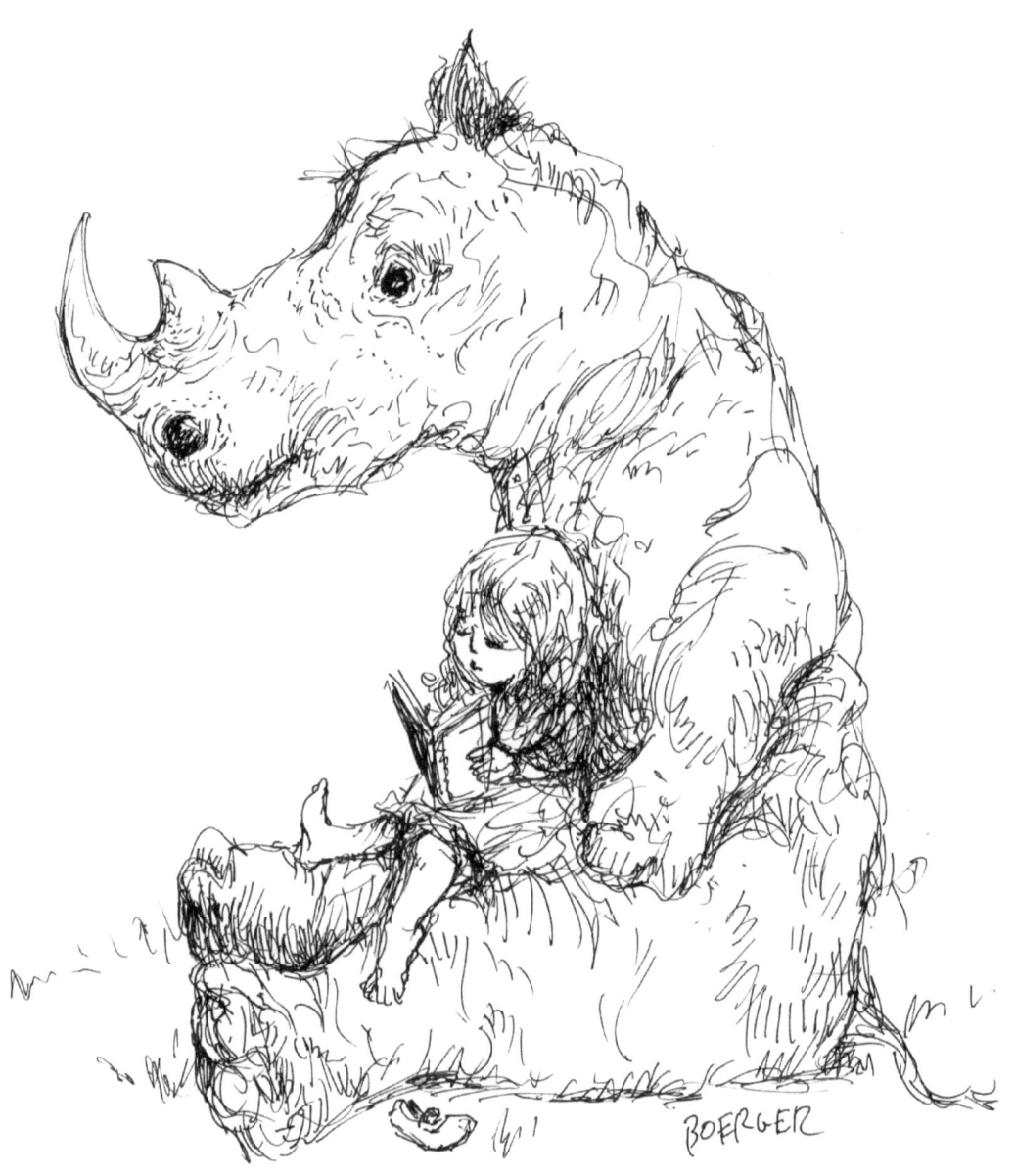

Pete Repeat

Pete Repeat lives on my street.
He says the same greeting at every meeting.
"Hello, my friend! You're looking well!
How 'bout this weather; ain't it swell?

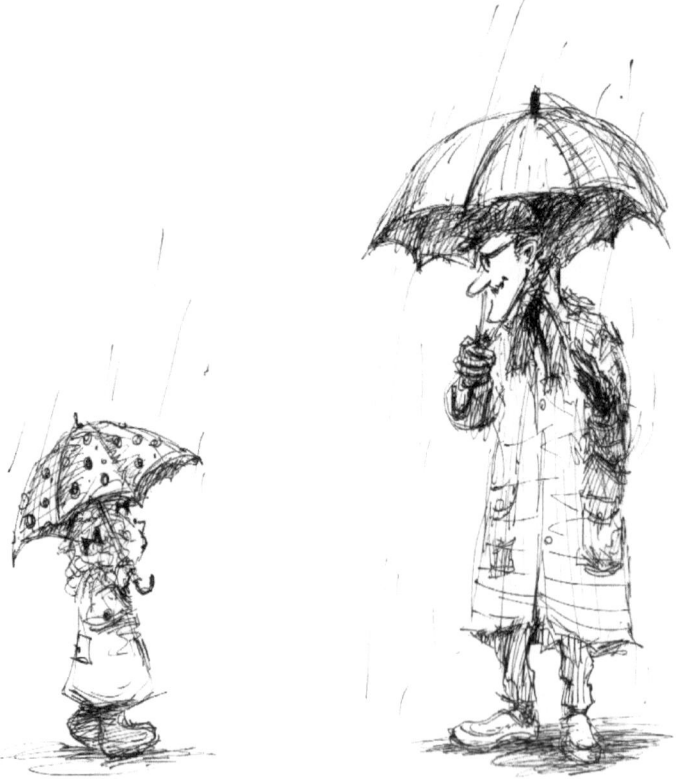

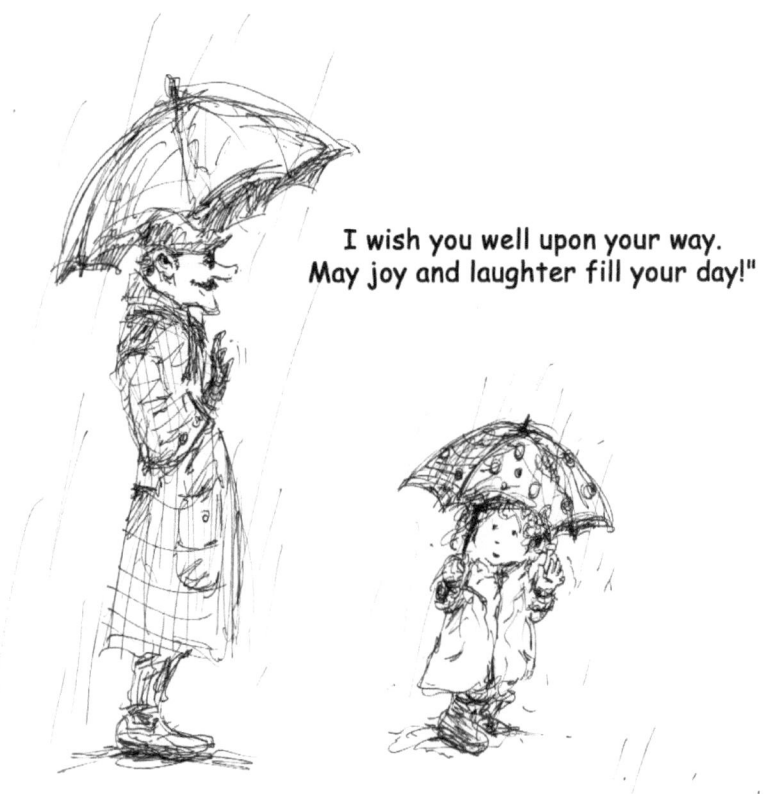

I wish you well upon your way.
May joy and laughter fill your day!"

The same thing every time we meet.
I'm very fond of Pete Repeat

Far Away

Would you like to know what I'm reading just now?
Not now, please. My mind's far away.
But *it's interesting!*
I'm sure.
and **fascinating!**
I've no doubt.
and mesmerizing!
well...

....will it cause me to know where this butterfly goes?
No, I suppose.
Then please save it till another time when
my listening mind is restored.
I will want to be
interested,
fascinated,
and mesmerized
then, but just now I prefer to be bored.

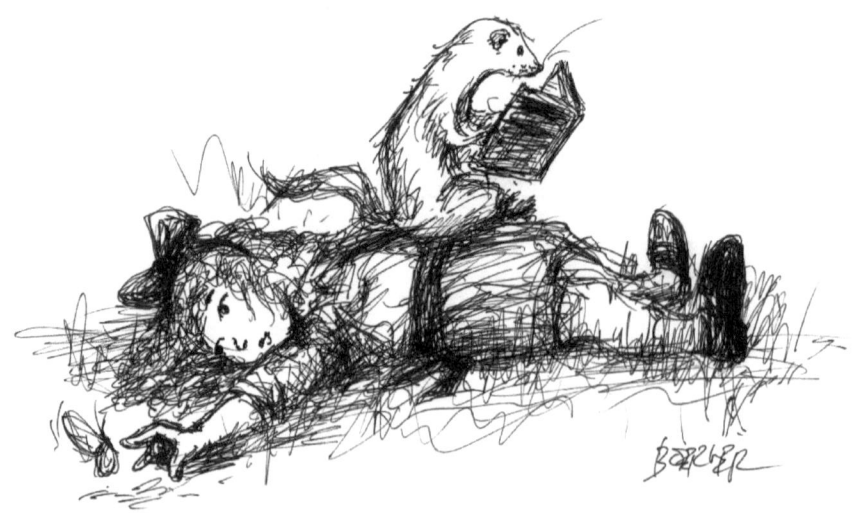

Gem

Hey, this is neat! Now here's a surprise!
You wouldn't guess it in a million tries!
???????
My name spelled backwards is 'Gem'!
Why, that's true!
How suitably, fittingly, perfectly you!

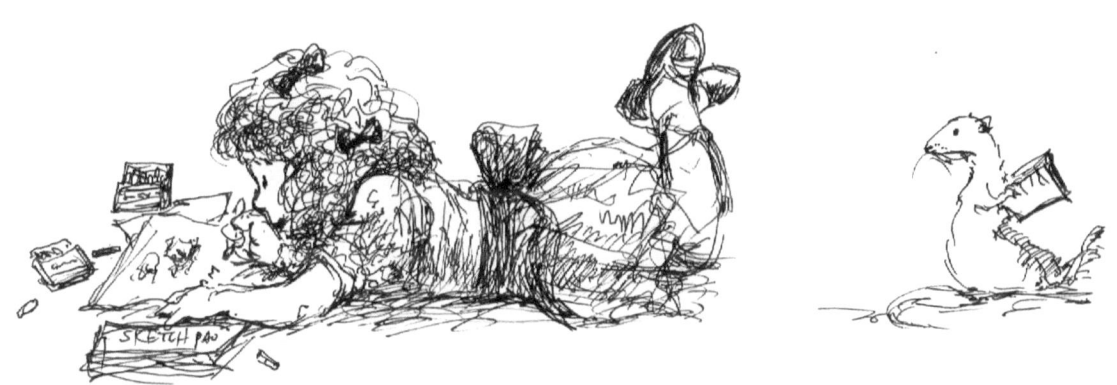

To The Zoo

I'm riding my trike to the zoo.
It's not what you might think.
I'm not going to ogle and coo
or make silly faces and wink.

The animals there; why, it just isn't fair
that they spend all day stuck behind glass.
They've done nothing wrong! And I'm certain they long
to be running around on the grass.

So I'm off to the zoo
to set them all free,
and bring them back home
to live here with me.

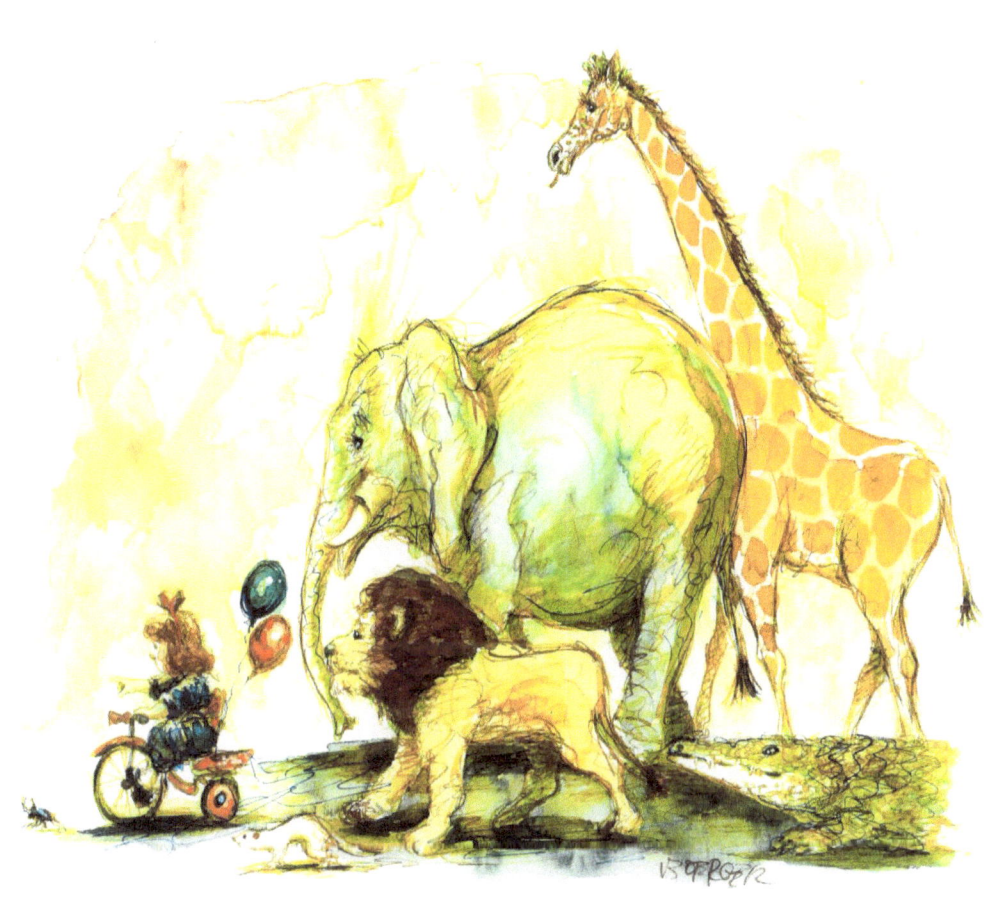

Two Wheeler

I simply don't see the point of this thing!
I'm fine just as I am with my trike.
With its sturdy three wheels it can hold itself up,
but you can't say the same for a bike!
How can my legs, just turning around,
keep something *up* that's supposed to be *down?*

Not for me, thanks;
I'm not ready, I fear.
I'm keeping my trike for
at least one more year.

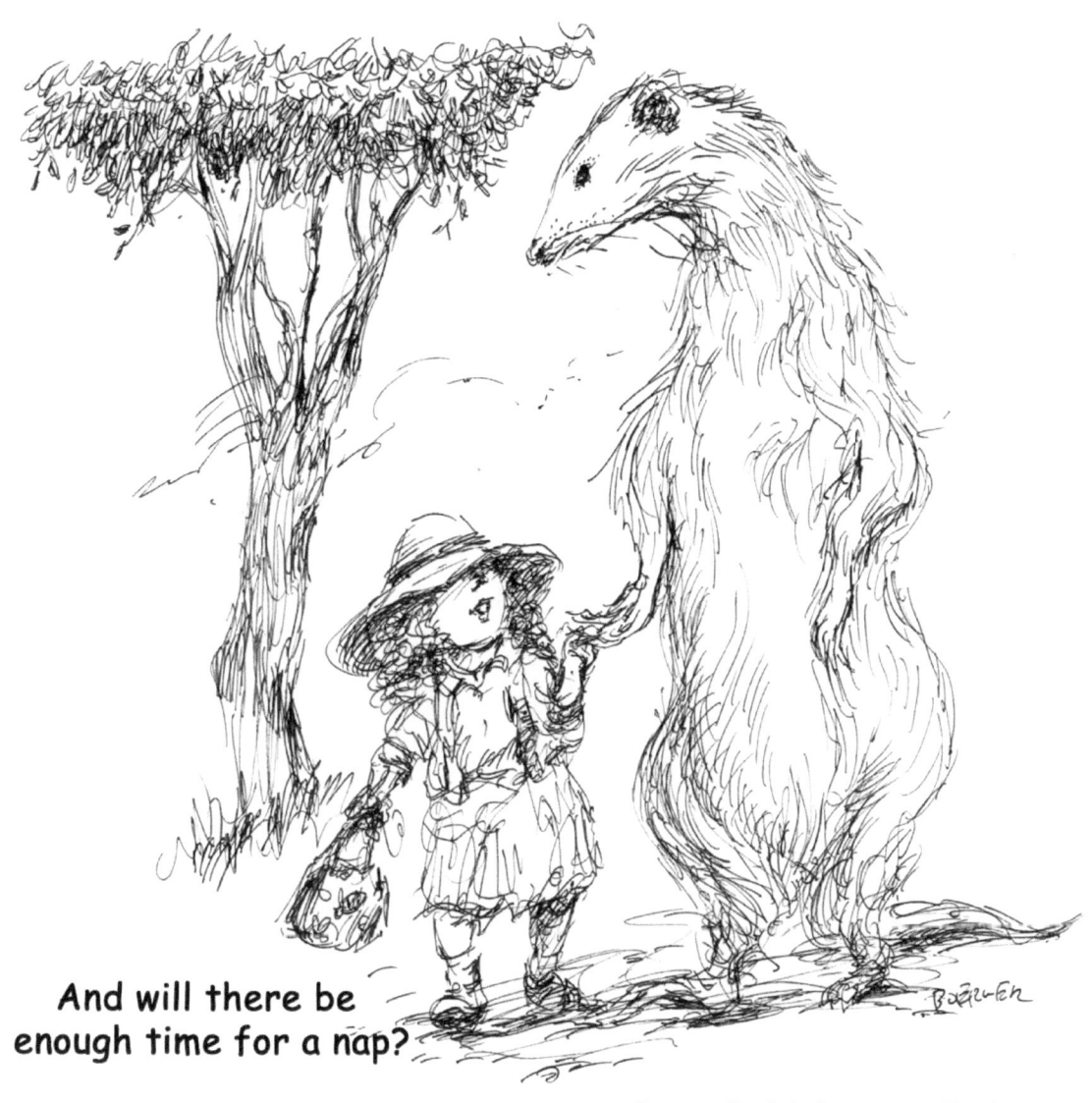

And will there be
enough time for a nap?

Dear Child, there will always
be enough time for a nap.

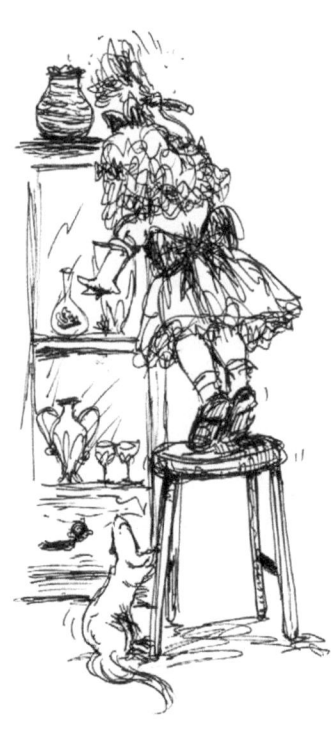

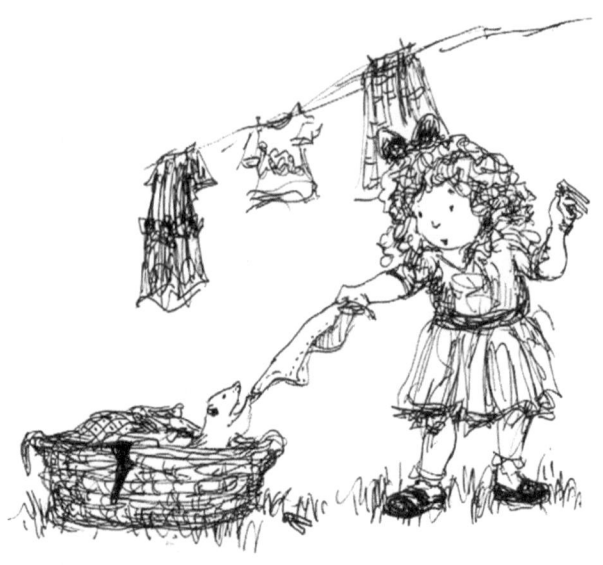

Things To Do

I've got plenty of things to do today!
Yes, plenty of things to do today!
Plenty of....(twenty of?) Far too many of!
things to do today!

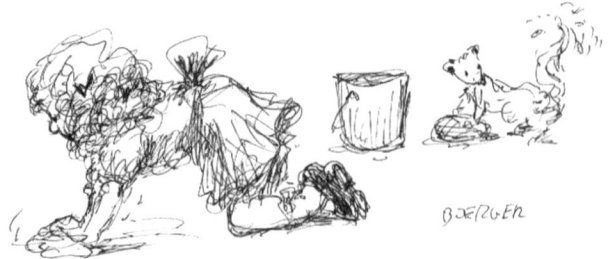

A Hike

I told you we shouldn't have passed through those trees!
But they seemed so far apart.
You'll just have to get better at spotting their work,
as they practice a secretive art.

Now your whiskers and fur are all sticky and gross
and my hair is in great disarray.
For we're both of us covered with spidery threads;
we'll be pulling them off half the day!
(and that means less time for play!)

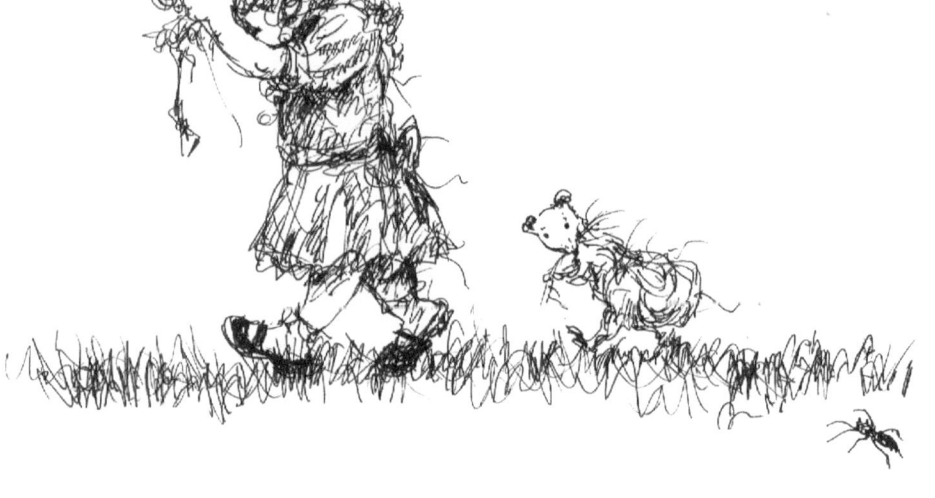

The Turtlebug

Among all the creatures you'll find
the Turtlebug's one of a kind!
When you look at his face nothing seems out of place
but when viewed from be-front to behind
you'll soon note he sports features
of 2 different creatures!
But that works out nicely, in fact;

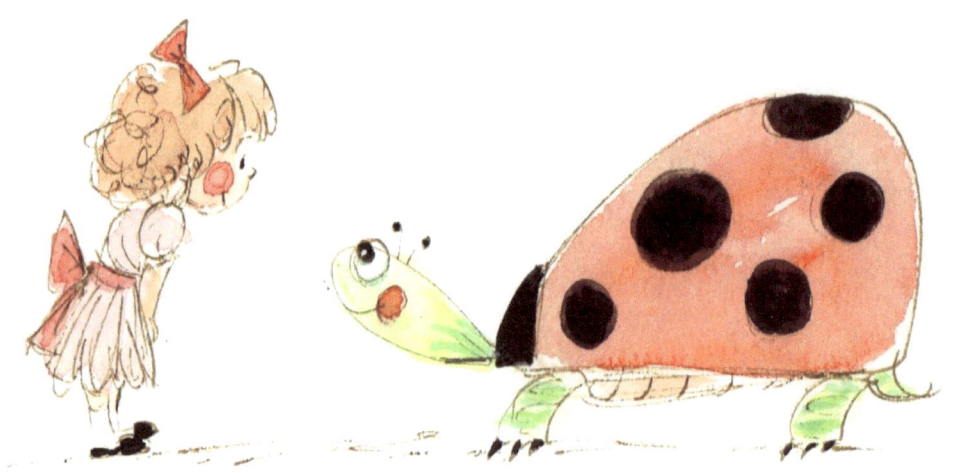

because when he flies he is just the right size
to take me for a ride on his back!

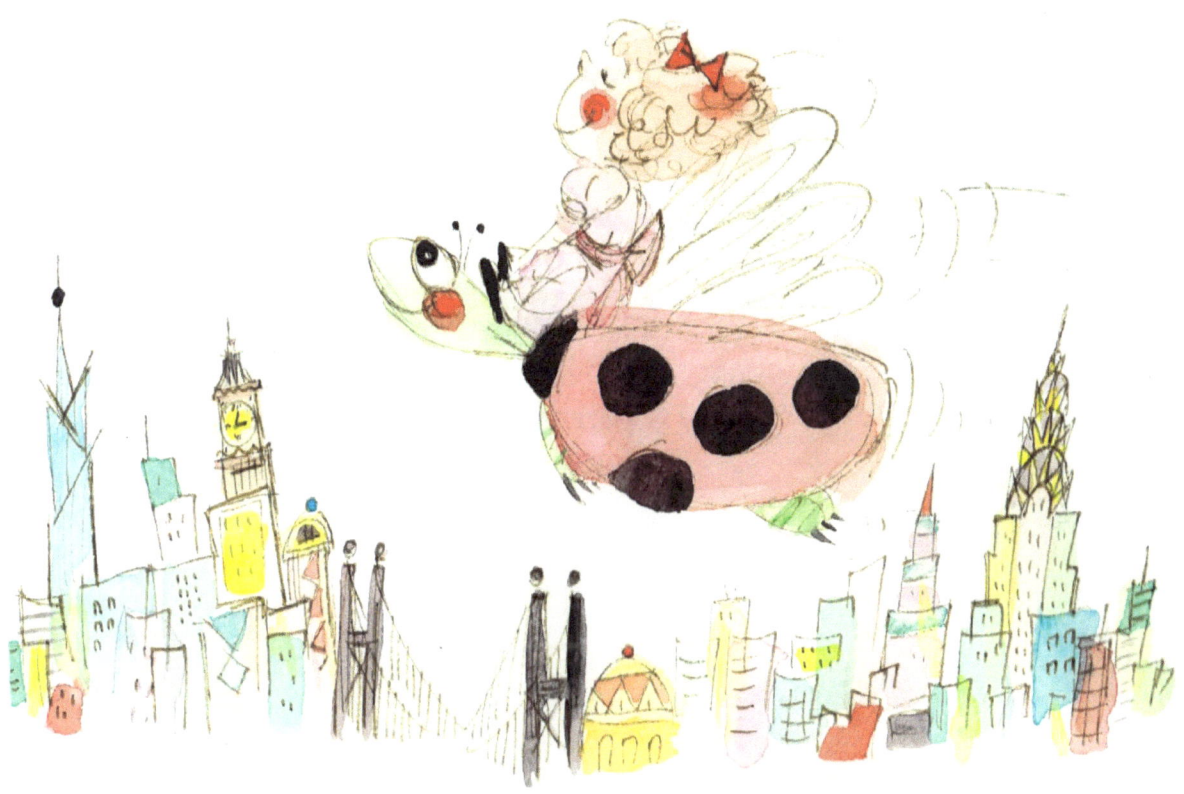

Butter The Stray

Butter the Stray, Butter the Stray
what sort of mood are you in today?
Will you grin a cat grin
as I tickle your chin,
or will you just walk away?

One never knows
with Butter the Stray.
But that's how it goes
with Butter the Stray.

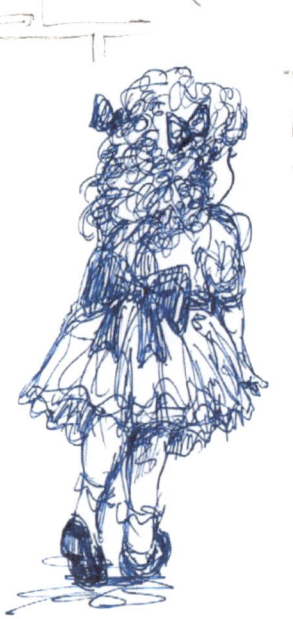

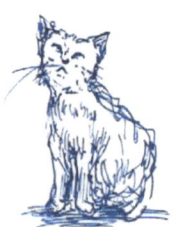

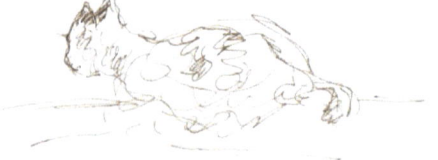

Swimming

Are ferrets good at swimming?
We're the best, though I don't like to boast.
Then, how would you like to go swimming with me?
Well, I'd like that the absolute most!
The problem's the pool has a very strict rule
about animals being kept out.
How's *that* for a snub?
Then let's just use the tub;
you can bathe while I swim all about!
(and we'll have even more fun, no doubt!)

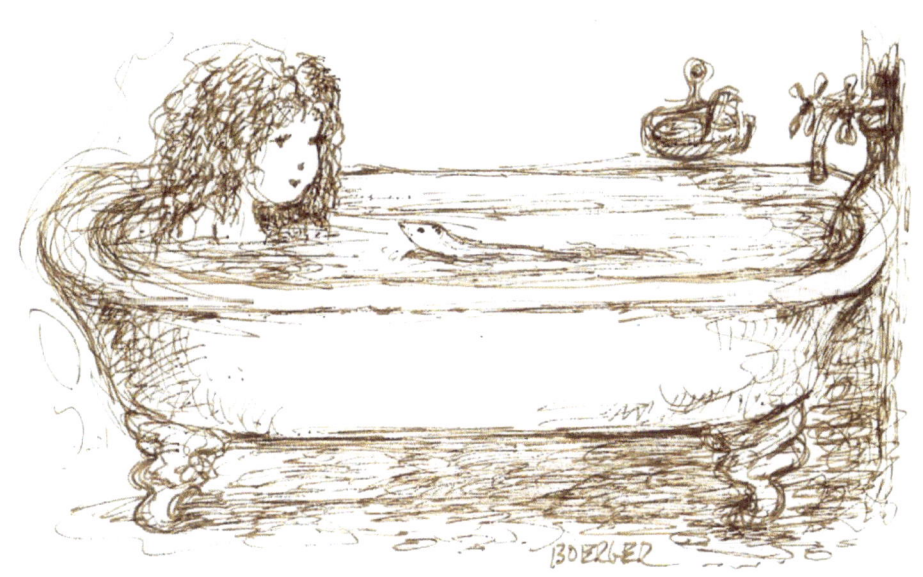

New Book To Read

I need a new book to read;
one that will sink into me
and show me a sign that all is in line
and give me a new way to see.

I need a new book to read;
one that will set me free
with words that are new,
so fresh and so true
they leap off the page into me!

Indeed, indeed;
that's just what I need!
A new book to read
is just what I need!

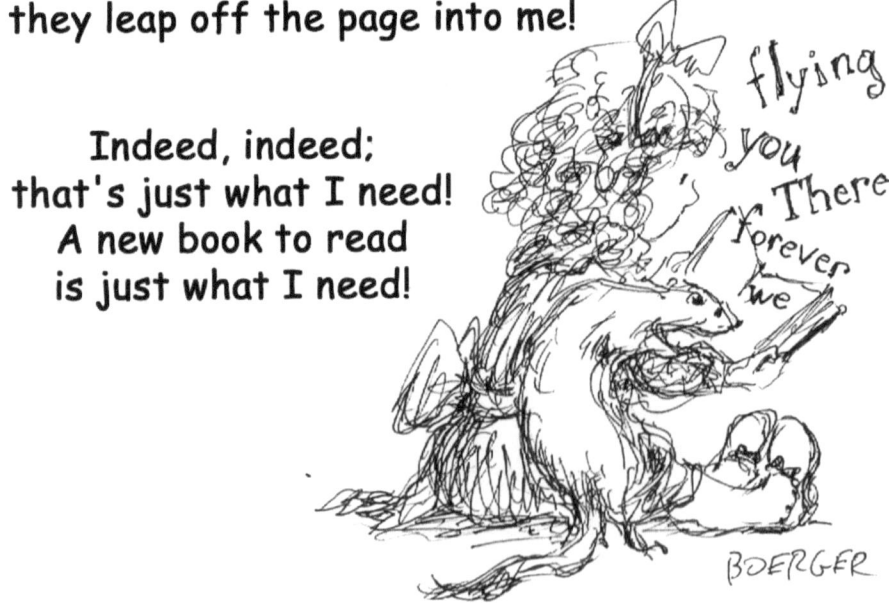

flying
you
There
forever
we

BOERGER

New Song to Sing

I need a new song to sing;
one that tells everything
with words that inspire,
and higher and higher
fly up like a bird on the wing.

I need a new song to sing;
to rise up above the din
and give people hope
and help them to cope
with whatever mess they are in.

Indeed, indeed;
that's just what I need!
A new song to sing
is just what I need!

bird
sun
garden
love

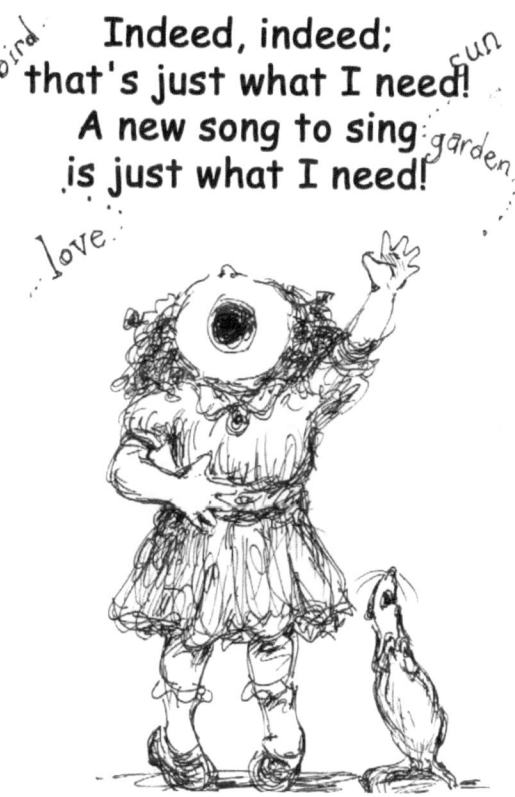

All today on a horse I shall ride
and my mom's eyes will surely grow wide
as we pass near the top of the stairs
and she gingerly steps to the side.

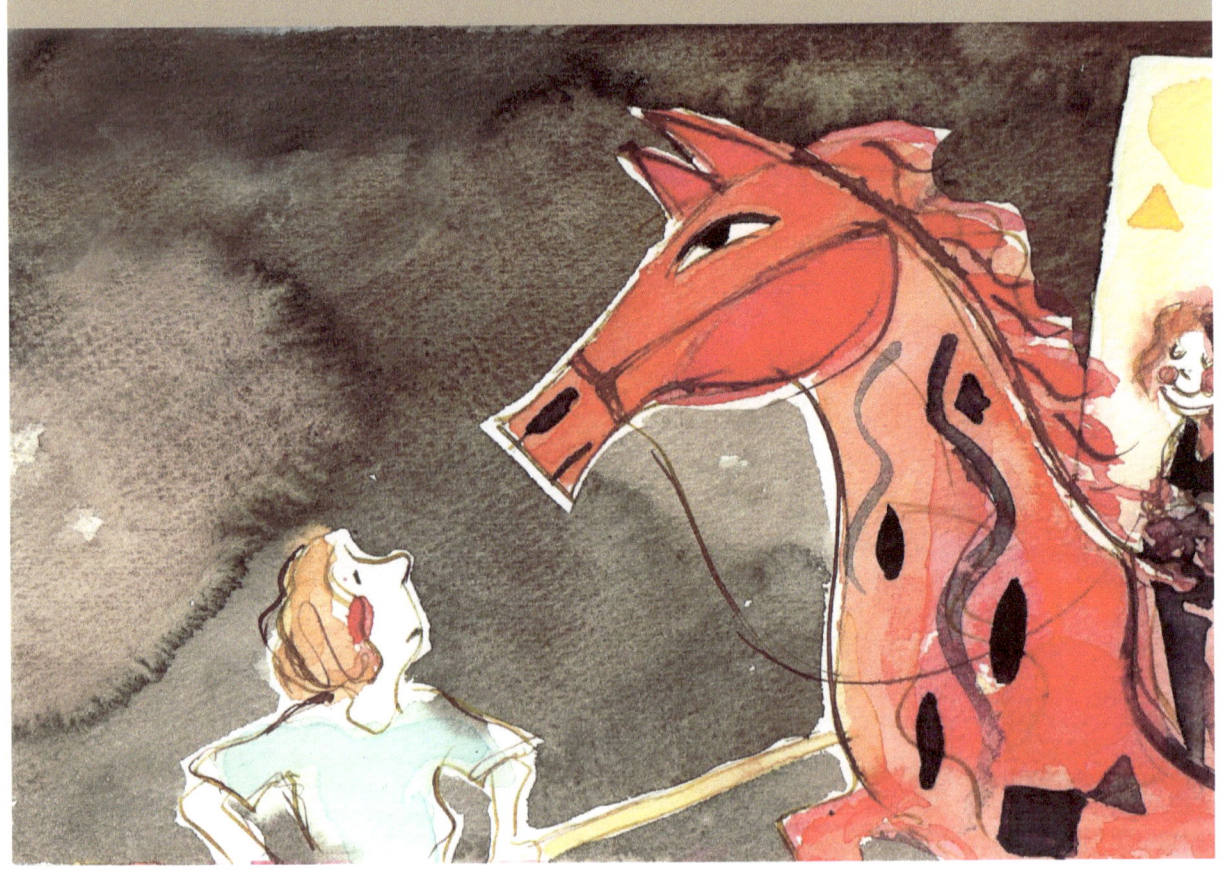

I shall breakfast on toast and on tea
while my daddy stares upward at me.
I am sure to appear rather odd
from an angle he usually can't see.

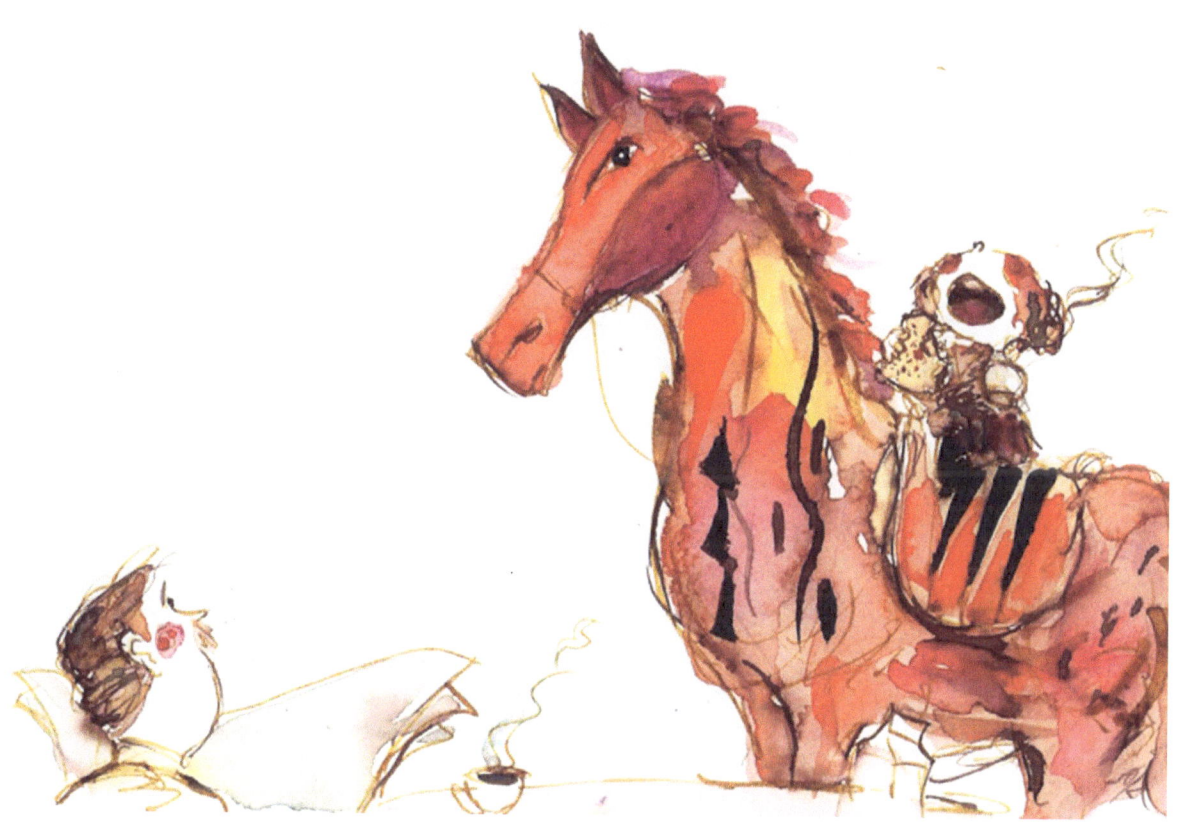

My big brother won't think to be mean
as he sees me approach like a queen
he'll not dare pull my hair on this day
if he *tries*, he'll be in for a scene!

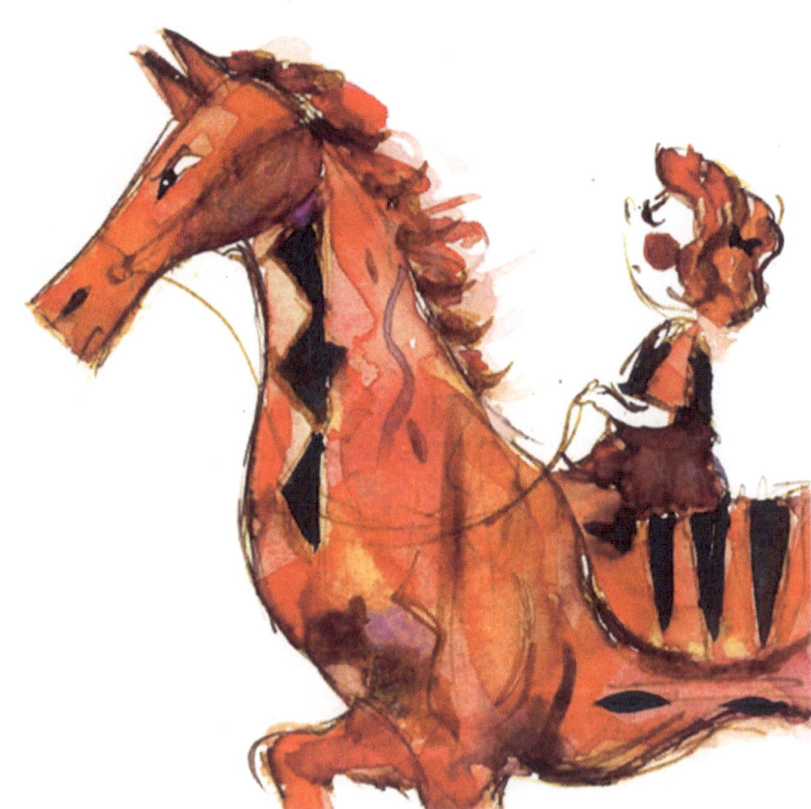

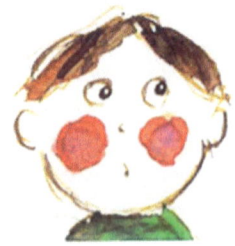

I will fly past my school-headed friends
as they go by the typical trends
of skateboard or scooter or bike
or a lift in the family Benz.

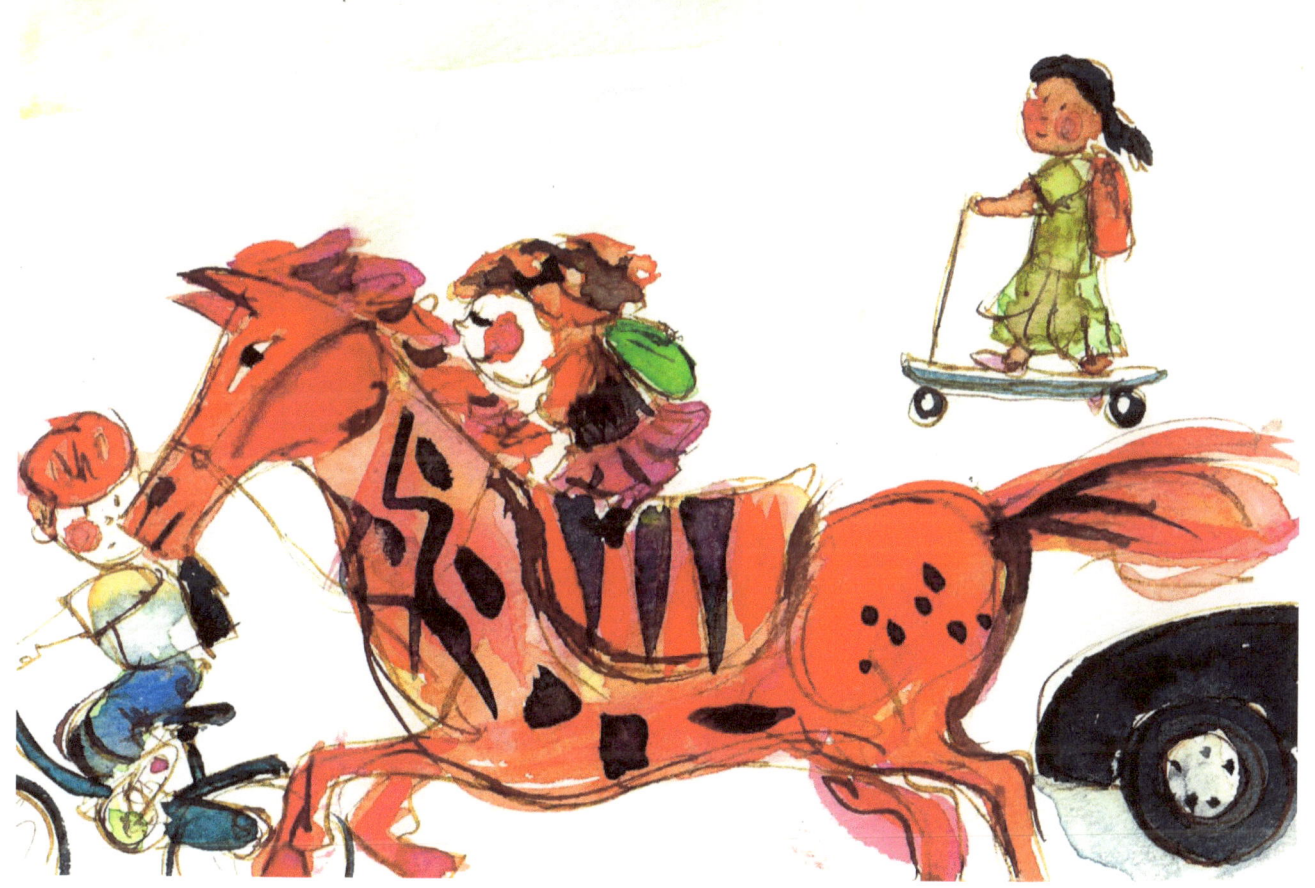

With my classmates at recess I'll play
and I'm certain to carry the day
I may manage a slam dunk or two
while the other kids all shout "hooray!"

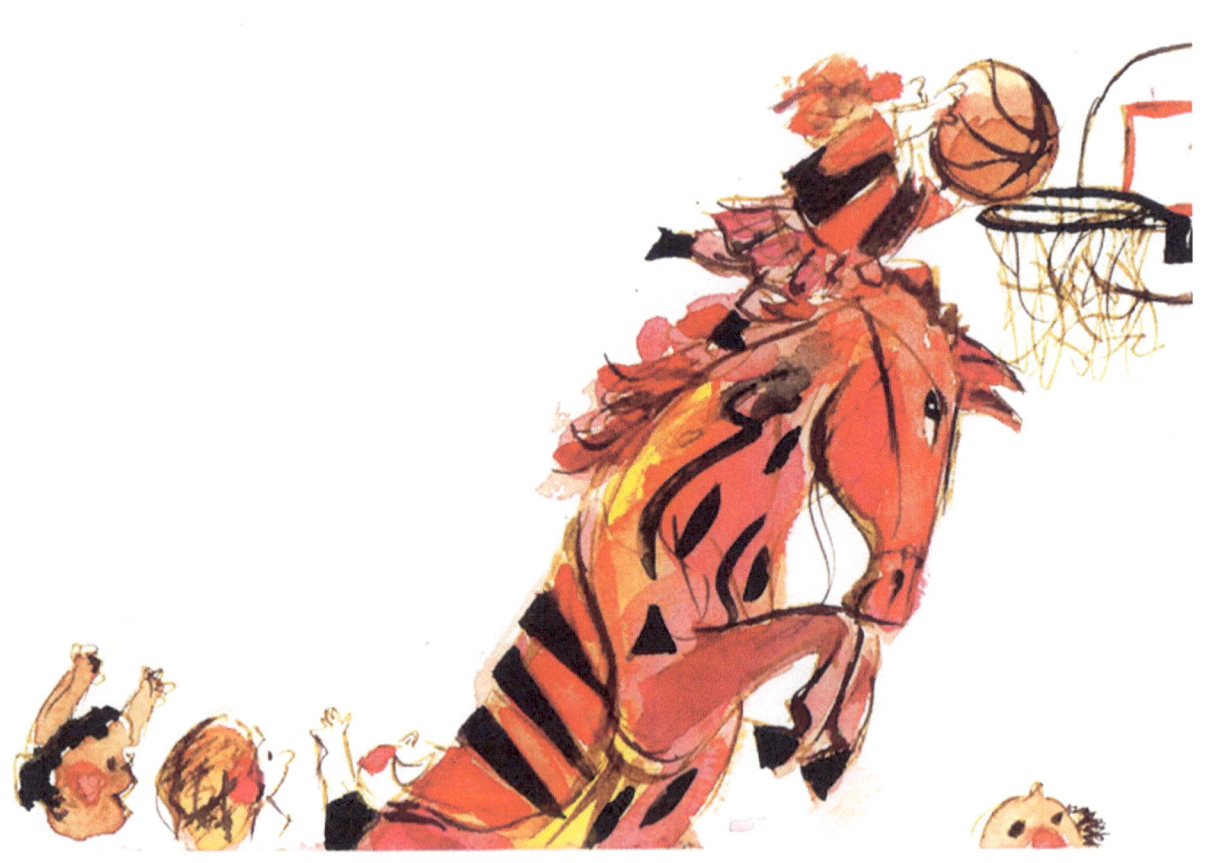

I will keep my horse with me at school
for I'm quite sure there isn't a rule
stipulating a girl can't recite
from a horse (or a camel or mule.)

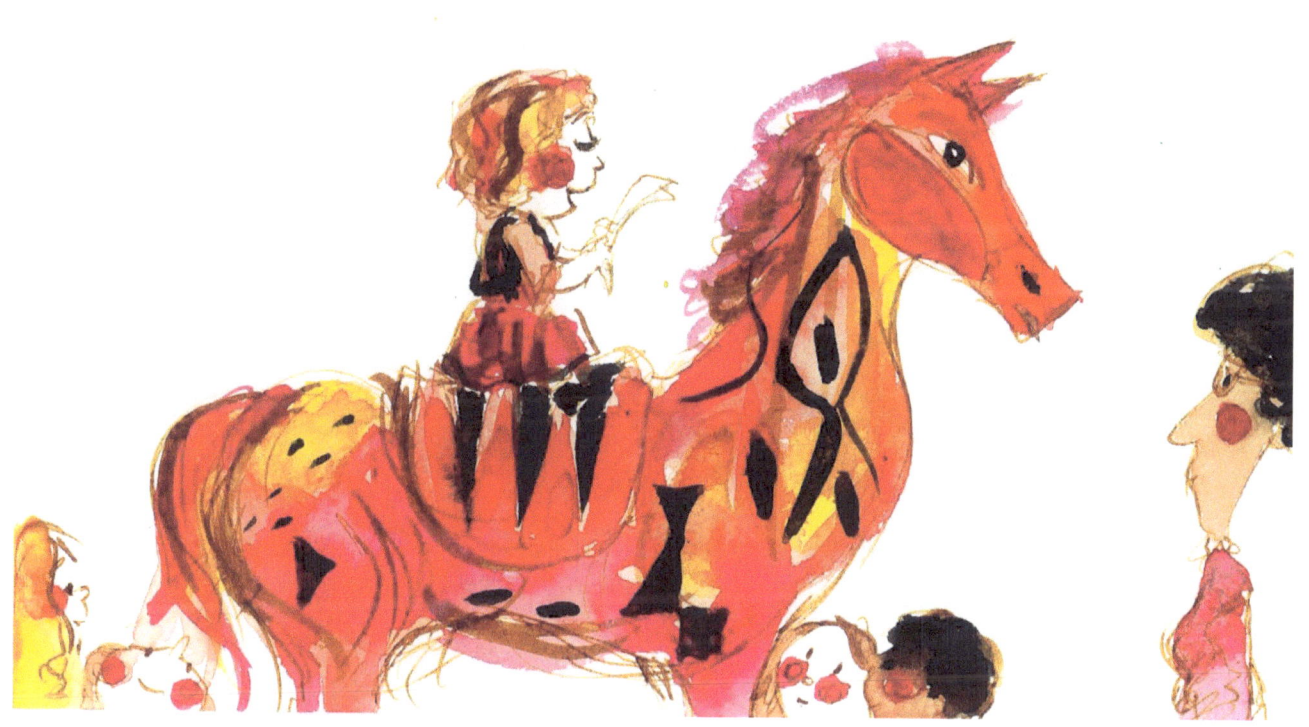

I will offer a ride home to Faye
for her house is just right on my way
it is likely to scare her at first
but she'll come to enjoy it, I say!

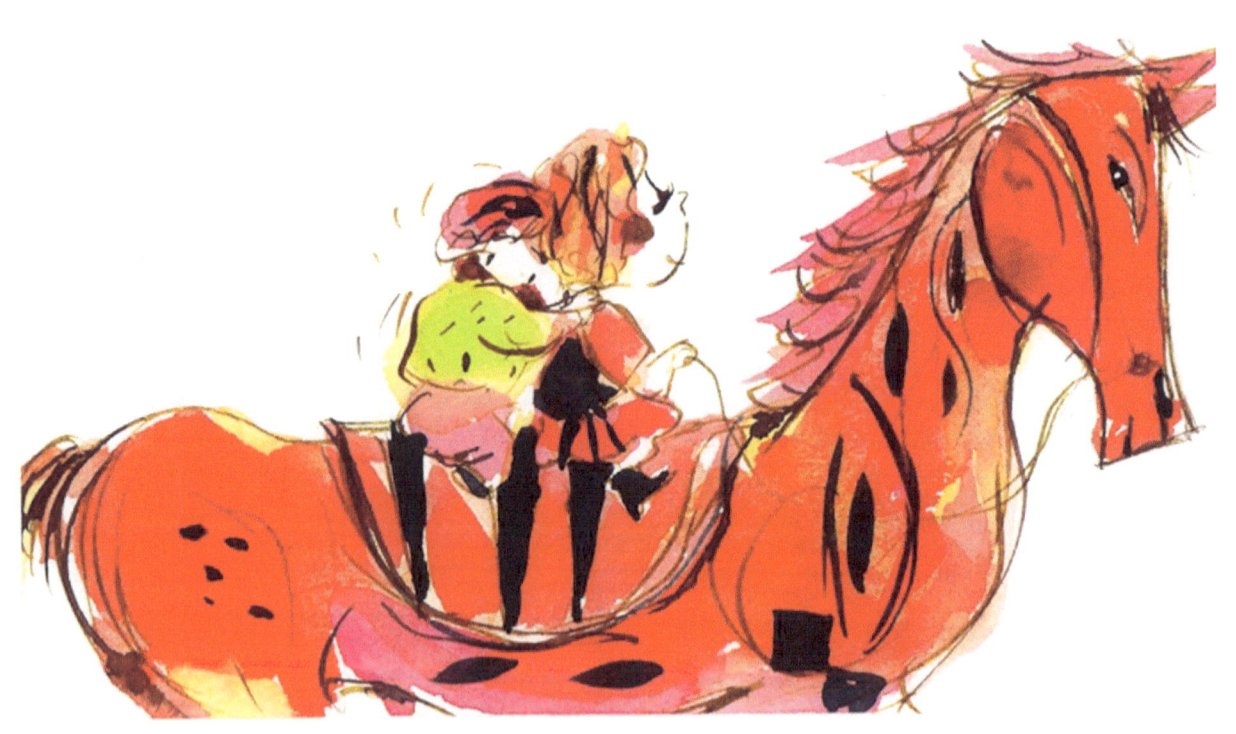

Though my homework's a terrible bore
I will gladly engage in this chore
for when done on the back of a horse
it is so much more fun than before.

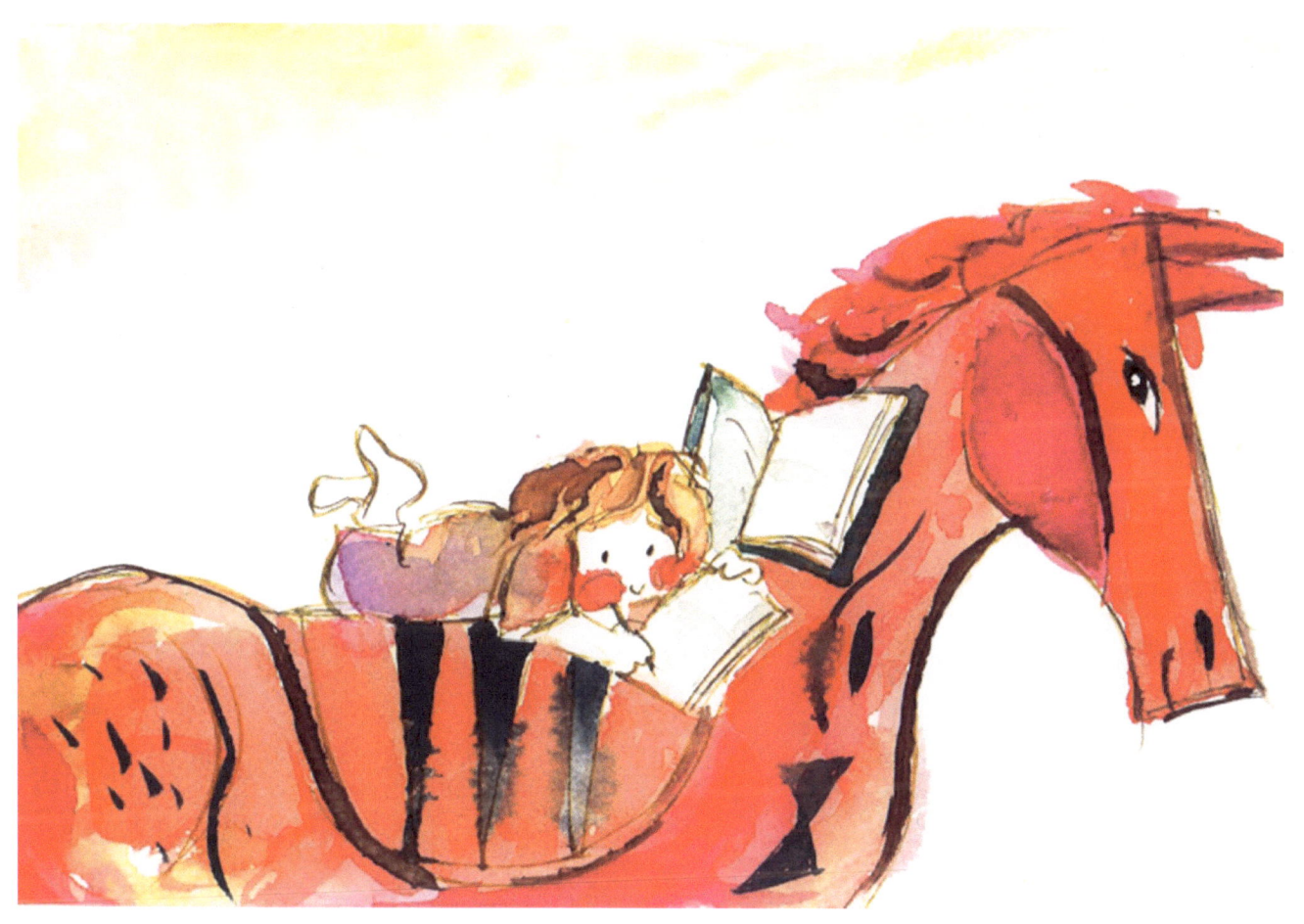

I imagine I'll watch no TV
for there's nothing on I want to see
while an evening ride under the stars
seems like much better time use to me.

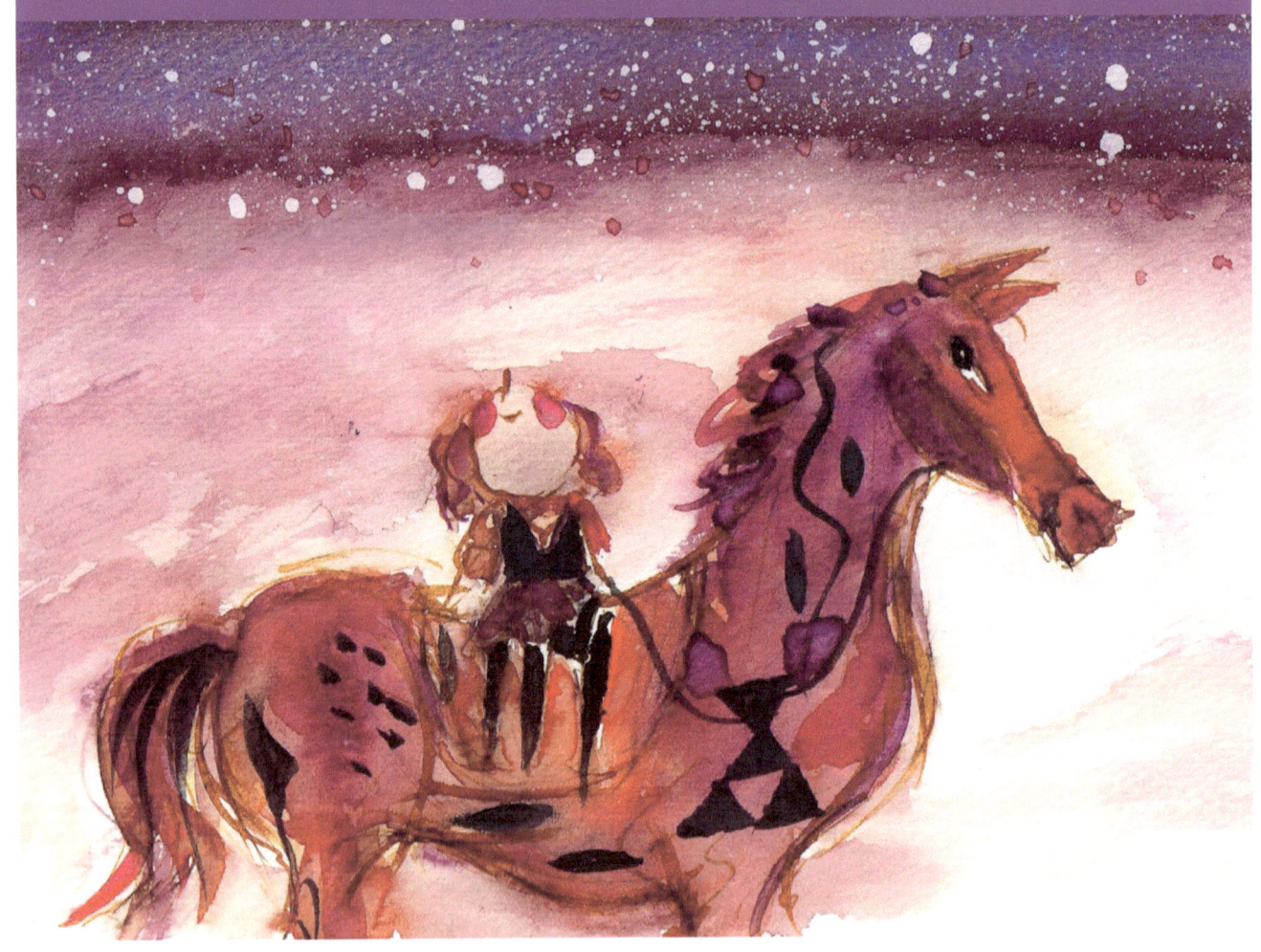

When it's bedtime I'll slide off my horse
for his hide is a trifle too coarse
as a comfortable place to retire,
so I'll sleep in my own bed, of course!

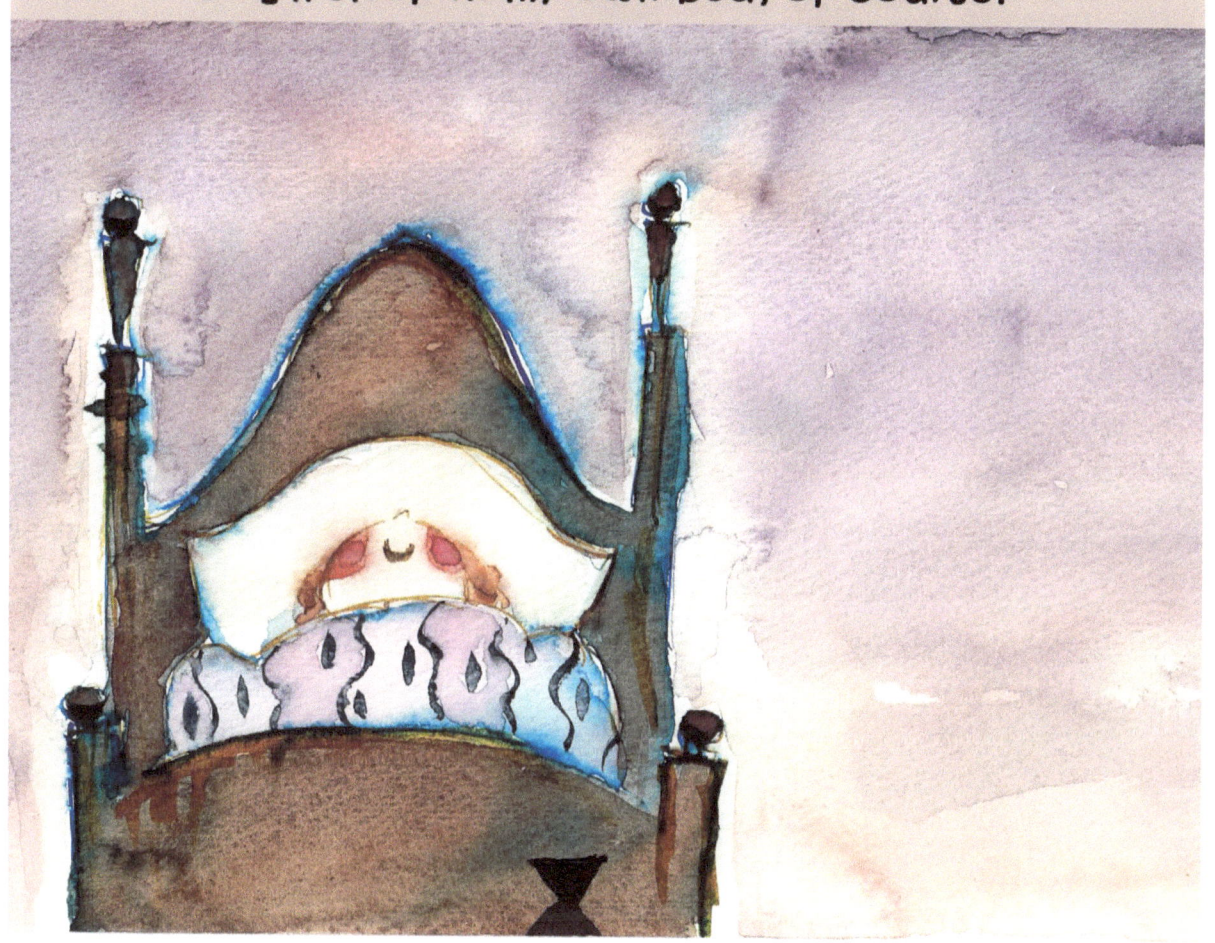

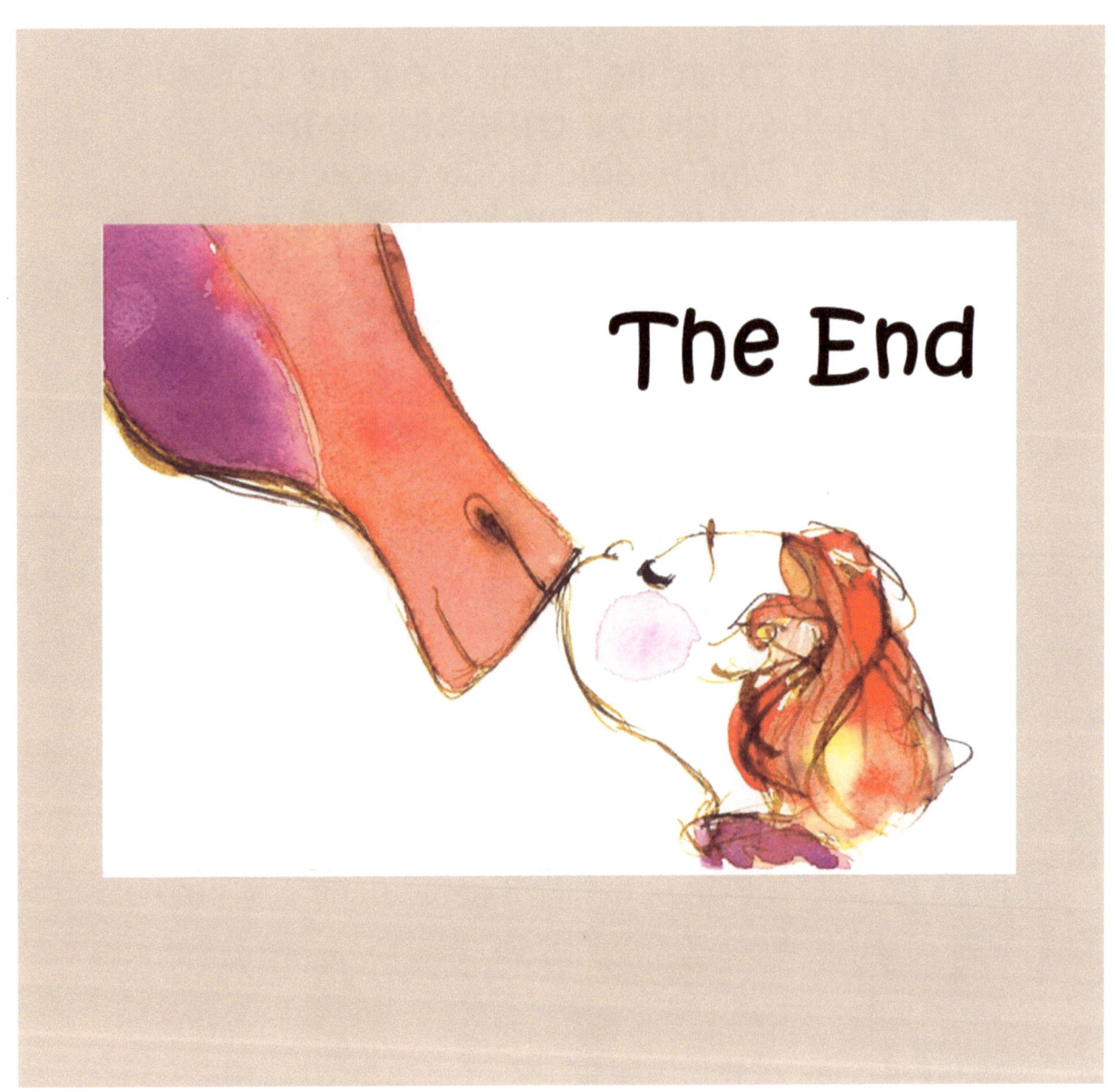

The End

Tea

He prefers things that are salty, while
I prefer things that are sweet.
So it goes that we often compete
when deciding upon what to eat
for our everyday's afternoon treat.
But there's one thing on which we agree.
We are both very partial to tea!

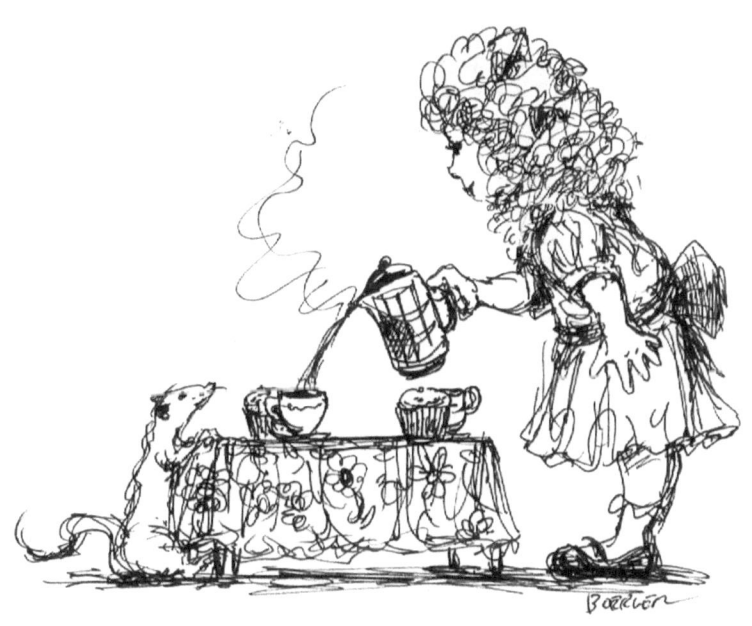

Special

Do you s'pose that I'll ever be special?
You *are* special, to me.   Yes, I know.
But what I mean is reeeaaallly special,
like the star of a musical show!

Oh...heavens.
If you ask me, such 'special' is way overrated,
and in chasing it down, you will seldom be sated.
Just be you, Meg, and do what you do, Meg.
Things that you find worthwhile, and that give you a smile.
Then all of the *already* special you are
will sparkle, then shimmer, and you'll be a star!

Small & Tall

When I'm in a room full of grownups
I sometimes feel ill at ease.
They seem like a bunch of Tree People!
Why, I barely come up to their knees!

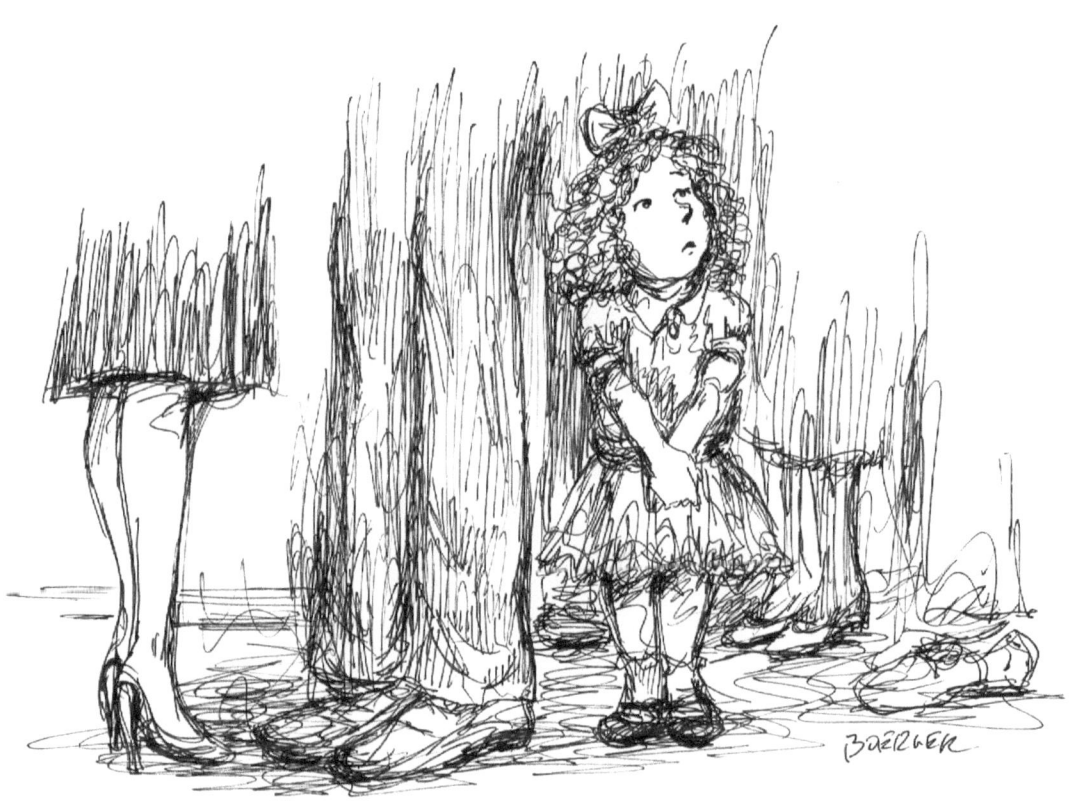

But I must seem like that to my ferret,
when he peers up at me from the floor.
I bet I look as tall as a building
that goes up twenty stories or more.

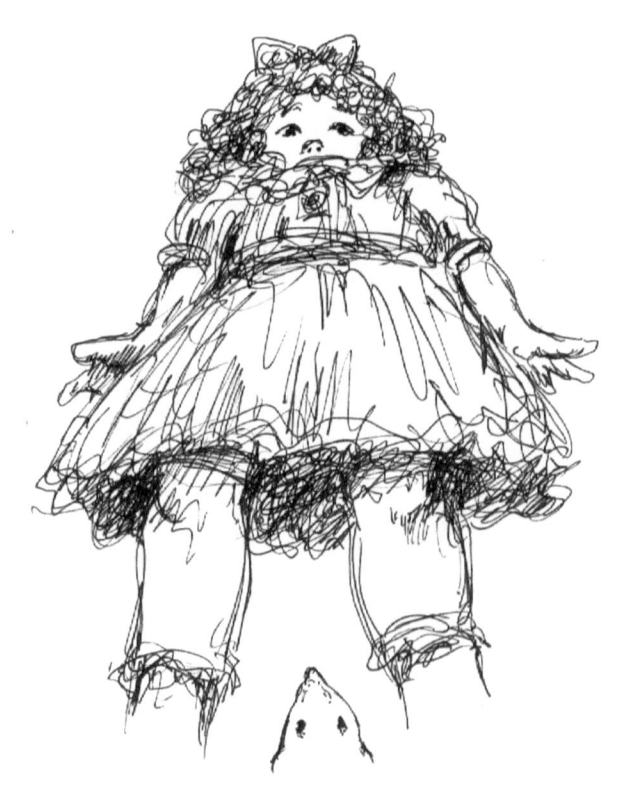

But...

don't feel sorry for him,
for he has his own friend, and to her he's as large as a tree.
She's the best little friend that a ferret could have!
And as tiny as she can be!

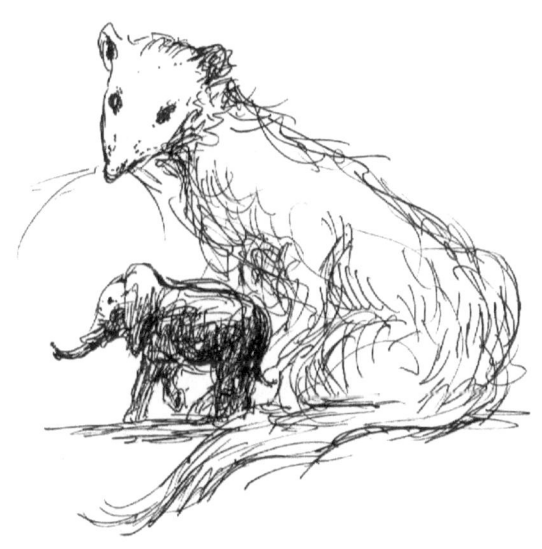

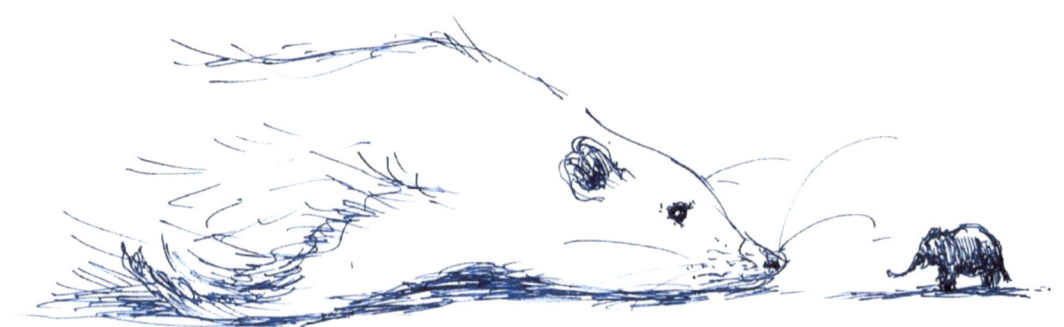

Race

What can these others be thinking?
Don't they realize this is a race?
If they try to hold onto all of their stuff
they will 'run' at a very slow pace!

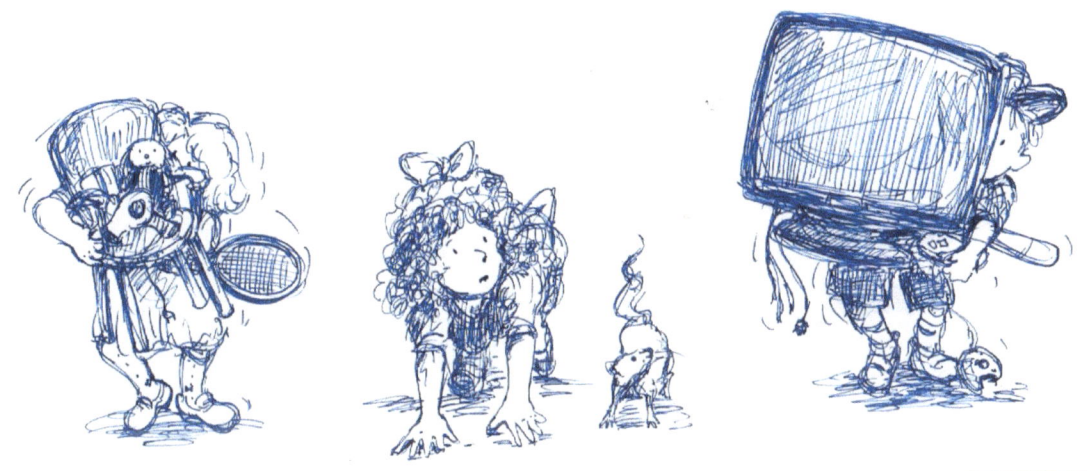

Let's just hurry along at our own breezy clip
and not worry a bit 'bout our friends;
they are sure to drop things one by one as they go
and end up just like us at the end!

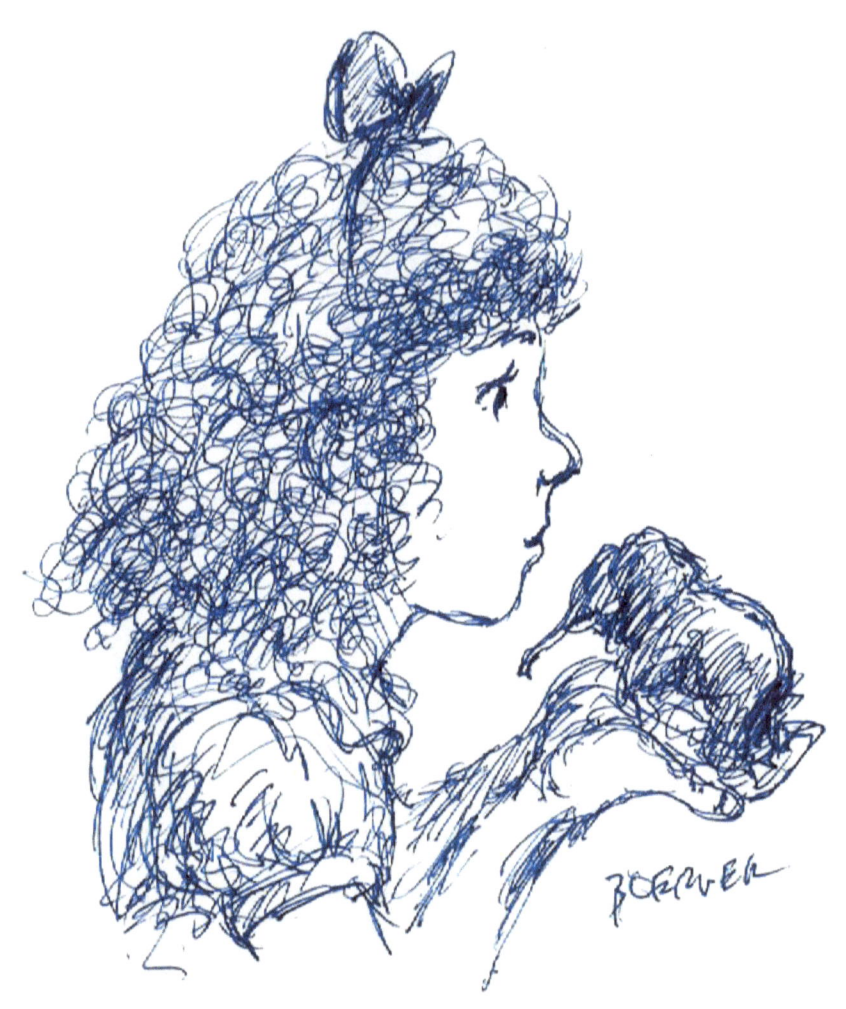

Success!

I learned how to ride a two wheeler!
It was easier than I thought.
My daddy was there, watching me with great care,
so I didn't fall down, a lot.

But my elbows and knees are a little bit sore
since they haven't been used in this manner before.
Tomorrow I'm planning to practice some more,
but I just want to sleep now; I've earned every snore!

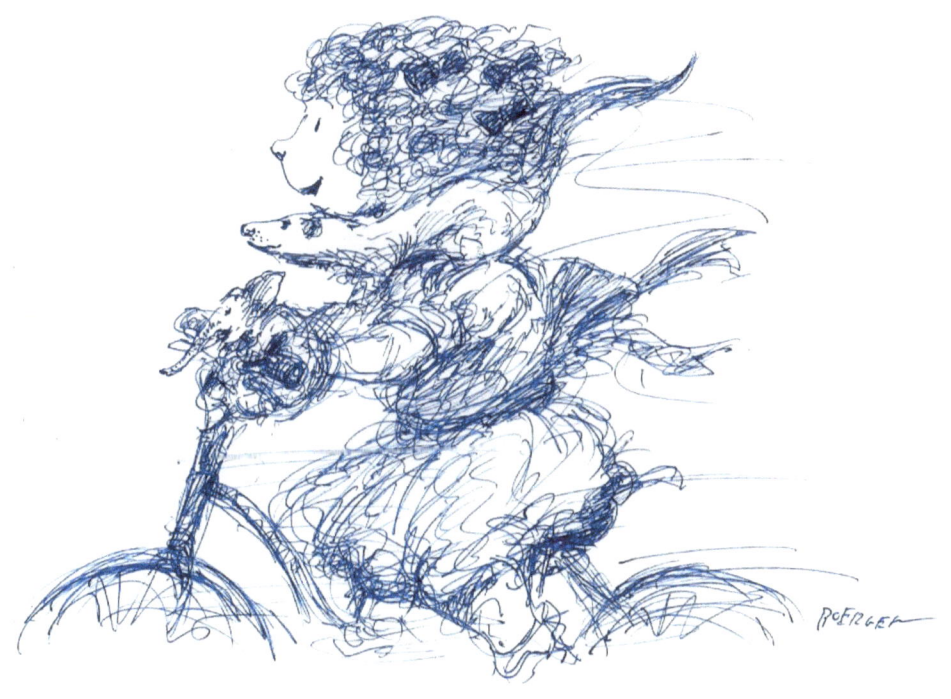

Life Is A Visitor

Life is a visitor, and a traveler.
It arrives, renting slender slivers of flesh for precious snippets of time,
then moves on to destinations unknown.
During its stay, it makes new friends, acquires new attributes,
gains new experiences and takes snapshots of itself
that will always remain important to it.
It checks out, sometimes in a rush,
and sometimes after having stayed a very long time.
It leaves, but never ends.
We grieve its departure
from this or that sliver,
but we are never truly without it.

BIERGER

I'll just read one more story;
a short one to share with my friend
though he'll certainly be lost in dreamland
by the time I reach

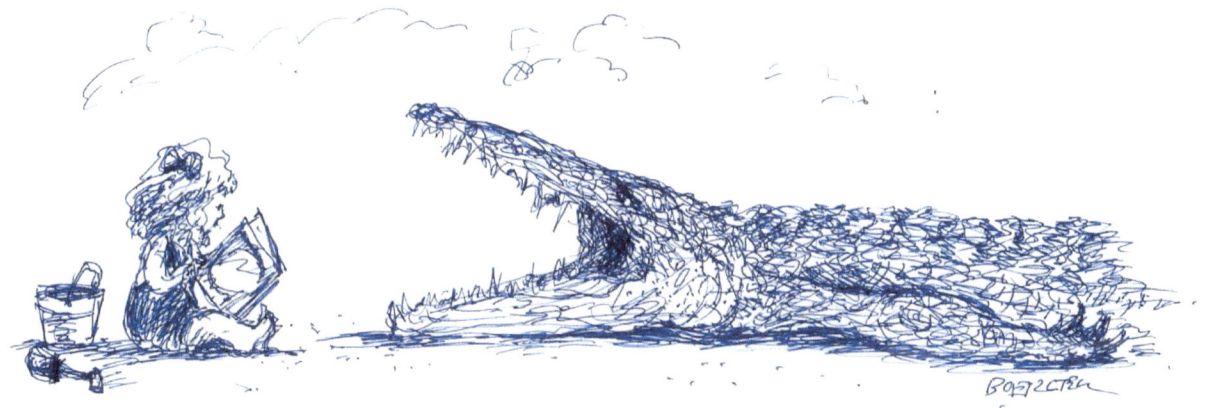

the end.

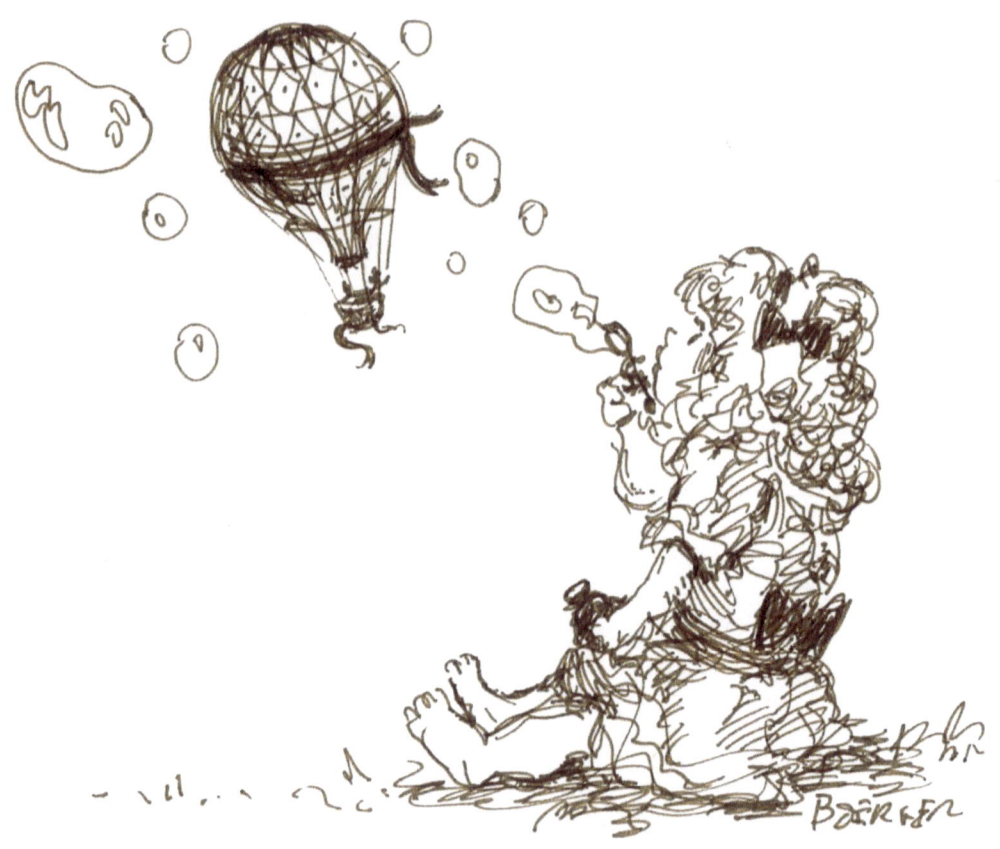

About the Author

I'm an illustrator/writer/educator from Columbus, Ohio. I have lived in Tokyo for the past twenty odd years. I've worn many hats throughout that time; though everything I've done ties into my passion for communicating, and creating. Combining words with images is a particular passion of mine. And children and animals are two of my favorite subjects for drawing, especially when the two interact in revealing ways. So this book sort of represents the tying together of many strings. I guess it's as autobiographical a book as can be, considering the subject is a very small girl and her very unique ferret!

You can keep up with me at my blog; http://andysart-andyboerger.blogspot.jp/ Hopefully, something for everyone there.

My illustrations appear in the book, *Sherlock Ferret and the Missing Necklace* by Hugh Ashton (with a sequel in the works), also by this publisher, and in the book, *What Does the Tooth Fairy Do With Our Teeth?* by Denise Barry. I will continue to produce my own stories as well.

I would like to dedicate this book to M.M., and to every child, adult and furry creature that has inspired me in some way that resulted in the book you hold in your hands.

- Andy Boerger

Available from Ted E Beans

(a li'l division of Inknbeans Press)

The Open Pillow, David Rowinski and Dea Lenihan
Digweed, the Cat, Eric Pullin
In My Sister's World, Ey Wade
The Magical Tree, Eric Pullin
The Travis Tales, Rose Salsman and Claire Turtlemoon
Dabby and Maxie, Robin Bee Owens
Sherlock Ferret and the Missing Necklace, Hugh Ashton and Andy Boerger
Tori-Jean, No! series, Jackie Williams
Read With Me, Pops series, Pops Burkett
God's Pinky Promises, Dawn Hood

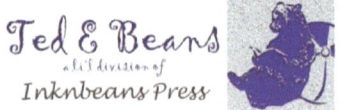